Lamborghinis

By Michael Green

C A P S T O N E   P R E S S
MANKATO, MINNESOTA

C A P S T O N E   P R E S S
818 North Willow Street • Mankato, MN 56001

Printed in the United States of America.

Library of Congress Cataloging-in-Publication Data
Green, Michael (Michael R.)
    Lamborghinis/by Michael Green
    p. cm. -- (High performance)
    Includes bibliographical references and index.
    Summary: Gives an overview of the history of the unique super car, the Lamborghini, describing some notable models.
    ISBN 1-56065-394-9
    1. Lamborghini automobile--Juvenile literature. [1. Lamborghini automobile--History.] I. Title. II. Series: High performance (Mankato, Minn.)
Tl215.L33G74 1996
629.222'2--dc20

                    95-27762
                       CIP
                         AC

Photo credits
Archive, 18. FPG/Howard Decruyenaere, 22; Chris Michaels, 41; Robert Reiff, 6. Michael Greene, 4, 26, 30-38. Unicorn/Jeff Greenberg, cover, 19, 25. VL Communications, 8-17, 20, 28, 29, 47.

Table of Contents

Words in **boldface** type in the text are defined
in the Glossary in the back of this book.

Chapter 1
Super Cars

Lamborghini is a famous Italian car company. Lamborghini makes the world's fastest super cars. A super car is a powerful vehicle designed like a race car. Unlike a race car, though, a super car can be used on public highways.

Super car owners must be careful. Police officers will follow super cars on the highway because they know they can go as fast as race cars. Owners of super cars must make sure they obey the highway laws.

Super cars are not **mass-produced** in factories like most cars. Super cars are built by

Lamborghini makes the world's fastest super cars.

Super cars do not look like normal cars.

hand in small numbers. Because of all the time and effort needed to build them, super cars are very expensive. Only wealthy people can afford them.

Super cars do not look like normal cars. Most super cars only have room for two people. Super cars are not designed to carry much luggage, either.

Most of the comforts found on typical sports cars are missing from super cars. Super cars usually do not have air conditioning, radios, tape decks, or CD players. The only important features on a super car are its speed and handling.

Speed and Handling

Super cars have low, sleek shapes. This helps them go faster. Most of them have air **scoops** and **spoilers**.

Super cars have big, powerful engines. They **accelerate** quickly. But power and speed are worthless if a car handles poorly.

Handling means more than merely steering a car. Handling means the way a car performs as a whole when it's moving. Super cars must have the right tires, brakes, and **suspension** system. Otherwise, the car will not handle well at high speeds.

Chapter 2

The Lamborghini Company

The company that builds the Lamborghini super cars was started by a man named Ferruccio Lamborghini. He was born in 1916 on a farm in Italy.

Even as a young boy, he was interested in all types of machines. His parents encouraged this interest. They sent him to a special school. Lamborghini learned how to fix and design different types of machines there.

Ferruccio Lamborghini started the company that builds Lamborghini super cars.

When Lamborghini was growing up, sports-car racing was popular in Italy. This sparked his lifelong interest in fast cars.

Farm Tractors

Lamborghini served in the Italian army during World War II (1939-1945). After the war, he returned to work on his parents' farm.

Lamborghini needed a new tractor to do the farm work. But after the war Italy no longer had factories that made tractors. Lamborghini decided to build one out of junk in his garage.

Lamborghini soon built more tractors using parts from **surplus** military vehicles. He sold his tractors to other farmers in Italy. His small garage grew into a factory by 1949.

In 1952, Lamborghini was building tractors equipped with diesel engines of his own design. By 1954, he was a wealthy man. He owned one of Italy's largest farm tractor companies.

To stay busy, Lamborghini entered the home and commercial heating and cooling equipment

Before Lamborghini made super cars, he made tractors.

business. Because of his energy, charm, and sharp business skills, Lamborghini's businesses were booming.

Collecting Sports Cars

Lamborghini had the money to buy almost anything he wanted. He began collecting sports cars. A sports car is a vehicle made for the pure

Lamborghini was not happy with his Ferrari sports car. So he decided to build a better one.

pleasure of driving. It is not a car made to take people to work or to the store. It is the type of car people drive on a nice warm weekend along a country road.

Lamborghini bought Italian sports cars including one built by Ferrari, an Italian company. He also collected sports cars from other countries, including a Jaguar from England and a Porsche from Germany.

Lamborghini Unsatisfied

Lamborghini was unhappy with the design and construction of the sports cars in his collection. Even his Italian-built Ferrari sports car had many problems.

Legend has it that Lamborghini took his Ferrari back to the company to complain. He wanted to see Enzo Ferrari, the owner of the company. But Ferrari refused to see him.

Lamborghini considered this an insult. He decided to build a better car than Ferrari. Lamborghini wanted the best and brightest car designers. He recruited designers from other Italian car makers. This was the start of a new family of Italian sports cars.

Chapter 3

The First Cars

Lamborghini's first car was simple, beautiful, and reliable. It was called the 350 GT. The first 350 GT came out of his factory in 1964. The body had been designed by another company. The **frame** and the engine, though, came from the drawing boards at Lamborghini.

The body of the 350 GT was made out of **aluminum**. The **V-12** engine was mounted in the front of the car. The 350 GT could go up to 150 miles (240 kilometers) per hour.

Lamborghini's first car was better-made than the Ferraris of that time. It was more interesting than any other sports car in the

The 350 GT was Lamborghini's first sports car.

world. Between 1964 and 1972, Lamborghini built 143 of the 350 GTs.

Lamborghini chose a fighting bull as his company emblem. He chose the bull because he was born under the **zodiac** sign of Taurus the bull. The fighting-bull emblem is found on all Lamborghinis.

Practice Makes Perfect

Lamborghini learned many lessons from building his first car. He soon designed and built an improved model of the 350 GT. This second sports car was called the 400 GT.

The Jarama replaced the Islero.

The Miura replaced the Jarama.

The Islero (eez-LEHR-oh) followed the 400 GT. The Islero was wider and longer than the earlier Lamborghini cars. It had a top speed of 160 miles (256 kilometers) per hour.

The Islero lasted for two years. Its replacement was the Jarama (yah-rah-mah). The Jarama was not a sales success for Lamborghini. Many buyers thought the car was poorly designed and too heavy.

The Miura

In 1966, Lamborghini built an **exotic**-looking sports car called the Miura (me-UR-ah. It was named after Don Eduardo Miura, a famous breeder of Spanish fighting bulls.

The Miura had a V-12 engine that was mounted sideways. This engine was in the middle of the car, between the driver's seat and the rear wheels. The luggage space was under the front hood of the Miura.

The Miura was named after a famous breeder of Spanish fighting bulls.

The Miura was powered by a V-12 engine.

Most cars have the engine in the front. Some
have the engine at the back. In a racing-type
car, it is important to have the weight of the
engine as close to the middle of the car as
possible. This makes the car easier to control at
high speeds.

Later models of the Miura had a top speed
of 180 miles (288 kilometers) per hour. Almost
700 Miuras came from the Lamborghini factory
between 1966 and 1977.

19

The Espada was Lamborghini's luxury sports car.

The Miura was a magnificent machine. It was far ahead of the cars being built by Ferrari, Lamborghini's biggest competitor.

But Lamborghini was not content with the popularity of the Miura. In the early 1970s, he realized that he would have to create a new car to stay one step ahead of other sports car makers.

The Espada Luxury Sports Car

The Espada (eh-SPAH-duh) came after the Islero and the Miura. Espada means sword in Spanish. It combined the performance and handling of a sports car with the comfort of a luxury car.

The Espada could seat four people. It was made from 1968 until 1978. There were 1,217 Espadas built.

Like bigger car companies, Lamborghini often had more than one type of car in production at the same time. Some models were made for many years. Others were discontinued after a couple years if they did not sell well.

Chapter 4

The Countach

Lamborghini designed and built a number of different cars during the 1960s. None of them moved the public like the Miura. But not even the Miura was as popular as the Countach (COON-tahsh). The Countach is the world's ultimate exotic sports car.

The First Super Car

The first Countach came off the factory floor in late 1973. That was after more than three years of testing **prototypes**. The Countach had incredible performance, superb handling, and stunning good looks.

The Countach is the world's most exotic super car.

Countach is Italian slang for "Holy Cow!" Legend says this was the reaction people had when they saw the Countach for the first time. Lamborghini decided to use the expression as the name for his new car.

Lamborghini's engineers put the Countach's powerful engine in the typical front-to-back position. It was not sideways like the Miura's engine. But like the Miura, it was still behind the driver's seat.

The Countach has a steel frame with an aluminum body. The Countach was fitted with two **scissors-wing doors**. This gave it a low-slung appearance. To open, the doors turn upward and well forward of the car's passenger compartment.

The Countach was in production for 16 years. Then Lamborghini decided to move on and build a new vehicle. It was a difficult task. Lamborghini was replacing what is probably the best-known exotic sports car in the world.

The 25th-anniversary Countach had the classic low-slung appearance of the first Countachs.

Chapter 5
The Diablo

In 1990, Lamborghini displayed its replacement for the Countach. The new vehicle was called the Diablo. It was named after a legendary and ferocious Spanish fighting bull.

The Diablo shared some design features with the Countach. It had a mid-engine layout, a low-slung appearance, and the scissors-wing doors. The engine in the Diablo was a heavily redesigned version of the powerful engine found in the Countach. The Diablo, though, was larger and heavier than the Countach.

When the Diablo was introduced, Lamborghini claimed it was the world's fastest

The Diablo replaced the Countach in 1990.

The limited-edition Diablo SE30 was introduced in 1993.

car. Lamborghini said it had a top speed of 202 miles (323 kilometers) per hour. Independent tests at racetracks confirmed the claim.

But the Diablo did not accelerate as quickly as the Countach. The Diablo went from zero to 60 miles (96 kilometers) per hour in 4.9 seconds. It took the older Countach only 4.7 seconds to go from zero to 60 miles (96 kilometers) per hour.

Earlier Lamborghini models were designed on paper by Italian engineers. The new Diablo was designed with the aid of super computers. Today, all cars are designed with the help of computers.

New Owners

In the early 1970s, a worldwide oil crisis caused gasoline prices to rise sharply. Because super cars use a lot of gas, the sales of Lamborghinis dropped. The company began losing money. Ferruccio Lamborghini lost interest in building super cars. He sold the company to a group of Swiss business people in 1973.

The SE30's powerful and lightweight engine produced a top speed of 206 miles (330 killometers) per hour.

The first Diablos did not accelerate as quickly as the Countach.

The Swiss owners could not make a profit with the company. In the mid-1970s, the Italian government took over the Lamborghini factory. The Italian government then sold Lamborghini to a German company. The Germans could not make Lamborghini profitable either. They returned the factory to the Italian government.

In 1980, an English-French-Swiss company **leased** the Lamborghini factory from the Italian government. Lamborghini slowly came back to life. In 1987, the Chrysler Corporation, a car maker from the United States, took over the company.

Chrysler owned Lamborghini until 1994. Then they sold the company to Mega Tech, a shipping and manufacturing company from Indonesia.

The Diablo was designed with the help of computers.

Chapter 6

Safety Features

Like the Countach, the Diablo has been improved since its introduction. In 1993, a new four-wheel computer system known as Viscous Traction, or VT, was added to the Diablo. The Diablo cars fitted with this new system became the Diablo VT series.

The VT computer system increased the Diablo's performance on wet roads. The VT computer system kicks in when the Diablo's wheels begin to spin.

If the rear wheels spin on a slippery road, the VT system automatically transfers up to 40

The Diablo's VT computer system adjusts to different types of driving.

percent of the power from the rear wheels to the front wheels. This allows the driver to maintain the car's speed without losing control.

Computer Controlled

The VT computer system shows that safety is a priority with the Diablo. It allows drivers to select the kind of driving they will be doing. The computer then adjusts the car's suspension to fit the driving style.

Sometimes a driver might select a slower, soft-ride program, but then go faster than is safe for such a setting. The computer will automatically switch to a stiffer, more sporty program for the increased speed. When the driver slows down, the computer will go back to the slower, soft-ride setting.

Power steering also improves the Diablo's handling without sacrificing safety. The Diablo's steering system is speed sensitive. The steering is stiffened as speed increases. This gives the driver precise control at higher speeds. It also allows for easy turning at lower speeds.

Power steering improves the Diablo's handling.

The Lamborghini Diablo VT

The Diablo Roadster is a two-seater convertible.

The Diablo's **chassis** is made from strong steel-**alloy** tubes. The body shell is mostly aluminum, with some plastic and carbon **panels** to help keep the car's weight down.

To make the body stronger, the Diablo's roof is made of steel and is welded directly to the chassis. The door frames are made of pressed steel. The doors are made of steel alloy.

Diablo SE30

In 1993, a limited-edition Diablo was rolled out of the Italian factory. It was called the Diablo SE30.

The SE30 was designed to be as lightweight as possible. Steel and aluminum panels used in earlier Diablos were replaced by panels made of lightweight **carbon fiber** and carbon **composites**. Carbon-fiber seats replaced the padded leather seats found in earlier Diablos.

Because the SE30 was lightweight, it could reach a top speed of 206 miles (330 kilometers) per hour. It went from zero to 60 miles (96 kilometers) per hour in less than four seconds. To increase safety, SE30 designers added a fire-extinguishing system.

Diablo Roadster VT

The newest Lamborghini to hit showroom floors is the Diablo Roadster VT. The top of this two-seater convertible is made of lightweight carbon fiber. It can be removed by one person and stored behind the seats.

Like the regular Diablo, the VT has scissors-style doors. The VT's engine is the same engine found in the regular Diablo. The VT's leather interior is specially treated to handle all types of weather conditions.

The Diablo Roadster VT has a top speed of 200 miles (320 kilometers) per hour. On a racetrack, the VT accelerated from zero to 60 miles (96 kilometers) per hour in four seconds.

To protect the driver and passenger in case of an accident, the VT has a strong **roll bar** built into the car's frame. High-performance brakes are standard. These are similar to the brakes used in Formula 1 racing cars.

The Future

Ferruccio Lamborghini never intended to mass-produce cars. He was happy to build a few special cars for wealthy car buffs like himself.

This attitude has held true with Lamborghini's other owners. Even in the best years, the Lamborghini factory has turned out no more than 500 vehicles in a single year. The most common Lamborghini is the Countach. There are only 1,745 in the world.

Only 1,745 Countachs were ever made.

The future of Lamborghinis is uncertain. They are very expensive to build, especially in such limited numbers. This makes it difficult for the company to make a profit.

If Lamborghini disappeared, the highways of the world would be a little less exciting. But the Lamborghini legend would live forever.

Glossary

accelerate—to increase the speed of something

alloy— two or more metals mixed together for extra strength

aluminum—lightweight, but very strong material, used to build everything from cars to ships

carbon fiber—extremely strong, lightweight material, similar to fiberglass

chassis— frame of a vehicle on which the body rests

composites—alloys formed of non-metal products such as plastics

exotic—something unusual and rarely seen

frame—another name for a chassis

leased—rented by special contract

mass-produced—when goods are made in large numbers so they can be sold cheaper

panels—parts that make up the body of a car

prototypes—cars built for testing and show purposes only

roll bar—a heavy tubular steel frame mounted around drivers to protect them and any passengers if a car rolls over

scissors-wing doors—doors that swing up and out rather than sideways as in normal cars

scoops—large air ducts

spoilers—parts of a car, usually long, rigid flaps, that break the air flow to make a car handle better

surplus—goods that are left over when too many are made

suspension—the system of springs and shocks that supports a vehicle

V-12—an engine with twelve cylinders set in pairs at angles forming the shape of the letter V

zodiac—an imaginary belt following the path of the sun, divided into twelve equal parts, each with its own sign

To Learn More

Ackerson, Robert C. *Lamborghini, A Source Book.* Osceola, Wis.: Motorbooks International, 1987.

Flammang, James. *The Great Book of Dream Cars.* Lincolnwood, Ill.: Publications International, 1990.

Gabbard, Alex and Graham Robson. *The World's Fastest Cars.* Lincolnwood, Ill.: Publications International, 1989.

Leder, Jane Mersky. *Exotic Cars.* Mankato, Minn.: Crestwood House, 1987.

Marchet, Jean-Francois and Peter Coltrin. *Lamborghini Countach.* Osceola, Wis.: Osprey/Motorbooks International, 1980.

Marchet, Jean-Francois and Peter Coltrin. *Lamborghini Miura.* Osceola, Wis.: Osprey/Motorbooks International, 1989.

Useful Addresses

International Lamborghini Museum
3308 Broce Court
Norman, OK 73072

Lamborghini Club Canada
P.O. Box 543
Tillsonburg, ON N4G 4JI
Canada

Lamborghini Company Headquarters, USA
7601 Centurion Parkway
Jacksonville, FL 32256

Lamborghini Owners Club
P.O. Box 7214
St. Petersburg, FL 33734

National Automobile Museum
10 Lake Street, South
Reno, NV 89501

Internet Sites

Alexander's Lamborghini Web
http://www.csv.warwick.ac.uk/~bsuqg/
lambo/lambo.html

Automobili Lamborghini
http://www.lamborghini.com

Lamborghini Clubs
http://hfm.umd.umich.edu/SHOW/
lamborghini.html

The Lamborghini Diablo
http://www.bastad.se/~johan/diablo/diablo.html

There are several versions of the Diablo.

Index